G000244723

F*CK YOU'RE OLD

An Hachette UK Company
www.hachette.co.uk

Summersdale Publishers Ltd
Part of Octopus Publishing Group Limited
Carmelite House
50 Victoria Embankment
LONDON
EC4Y 0DZ
UK

www.summersdale.com

Printed and bound in the Czech Republic

ISBN: 978-1-78783-516-0

TO Jo & Roy

Love
FROM Sarah & Adrian
x x x

OLD AGE: WHEN ACTIONS CREAK LOUDER THAN WORDS.

DANA ROBBINS

IF YOU SURVIVE LONG ENOUGH, YOU'RE REVERED — RATHER LIKE AN OLD BUILDING.

KATHARINE HEPBURN

Age is an issue of mind over matter. If you don't mind, it doesn't matter.

Mark Twain

I STILL HAVE
A FULL DECK;
I JUST SHUFFLE
SLOWER NOW.

ANONYMOUS

At 70 years old, if I could give my younger self one piece of advice, it would be to use the words "f*ck off" much more frequently.

HELEN MIRREN

I am in the prime of senility.

Benjamin Franklin

ON THE WHOLE,
THE YEARS
HAVE BEEN KIND.
**IT WAS JUST
THE WEEKENDS
THAT DID
THE DAMAGE.**

I guess I don't so much mind being old, as I mind being fat and old.

Peter Gabriel

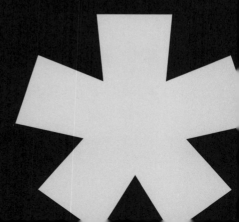

Act as young as you feel. You're not getting older; you're getting more entitled to be your fabulous self.

Gwen Stefani

WE MIGHT BE OLDER, BUT NOBODY SAID WE WERE WISER.

I KNEW I WAS GOING BALD WHEN IT WAS TAKING ME LONGER AND LONGER TO WASH MY FACE.

HARRY HILL

I DON'T NEED
YOU TO REMIND
ME OF MY
AGE. I HAVE A
BLADDER TO DO
THAT FOR ME.

STEPHEN FRY

THE ELDERLY
DON'T DRIVE
THAT BADLY;
THEY'RE JUST
THE ONLY ONES
WITH TIME TO DO
THE SPEED LIMIT.

**LET'S NOT AGE —
LET'S JUST
MARINATE.**

**People say
that age is just
a state of mind.
I say it's more
about the state
of your body.**

Anonymous

MIDDLE AGE –
A STEALTHY,
CRAFTY
NEMESIS.

TERRI GUILLEMETS

Give up being a
good example –
be a terrible
warning instead.

There's a vintage which comes with age and experience.

Jon Bon Jovi

HOW YOUNG
CAN YOU DIE
OF OLD AGE?

Old age is a shipwreck.

Charles de Gaulle

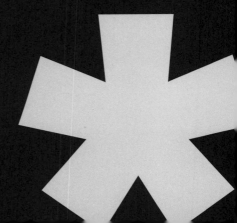

You know you're getting old when you're asleep before the time you used to go out.

I DON'T KNOW WHAT'S HAPPENED TO ME. I'VE GOT A BIT MORE SOPHISTICATED IN MY OLD AGE. I LIKE A BIT OF JASMINE TEA.

Danny Dyer

MY BEST BIRTH CONTROL NOW IS TO LEAVE THE LIGHTS ON.

JOAN RIVERS

THE SECRET TO STAYING YOUNG? LIE ABOUT YOUR AGE.

THERE'S ONE ADVANTAGE TO BEING 102. NO PEER PRESSURE.

DENNIS WOLFBERG

THEY TALK ABOUT THE ECONOMY THIS YEAR... MY HAIRLINE IS IN RECESSION, MY WAISTLINE IS IN INFLATION. ALTOGETHER, I'M IN DEPRESSION.

RICK MAJERUS

I want to live to be 120. That's when I will start worrying about my age.

Helena Christensen

WHY ARE
YOU GETTING
OLDER AND
WIDER
INSTEAD OF
OLDER AND
WISER?

When I passed 40
I dropped pretence,
'cause men like women
who got some sense.

MAYA ANGELOU

Everything slows down with age, except the time it takes cake and ice cream to reach your hips.

John Wagner

YOU KNOW YOU'RE
GETTING OLD WHEN
**YOUR IDEA OF
HAPPY HOUR IS
HAVING A NAP.**

Old age isn't so bad when you consider the alternative.

Maurice Chevalier

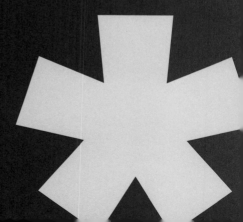

**The older
I grow the
more I distrust
the familiar
doctrine that
age brings
wisdom.**

H. L. Mencken

A DIPLOMAT IS A MAN WHO ALWAYS REMEMBERS A WOMAN'S BIRTHDAY BUT NEVER REMEMBERS HER AGE.

Robert Frost

AGE IS NO BARRIER, UNLESS YOU WANT TO GO ON AN 18–30 HOLIDAY.

THE WHITER
MY HAIR
BECOMES,
THE MORE
READY
PEOPLE ARE
TO BELIEVE
WHAT I SAY.

BERTRAND RUSSELL

THE SEVEN AGES OF MAN: SPILLS, DRILLS, THRILLS, BILLS, ILLS, PILLS AND WILLS.

RICHARD J. NEEDHAM

F*CKING OLD

IS FAR

BETTER THAN

F*CKING DEAD.

I tend not to think about living to some grand old age. Then again, I don't think about dying, either.

Stella Young

THERE ARE NO
OLD PEOPLE
NOWADAYS;
THEY ARE
EITHER
"WONDERFUL
FOR THEIR AGE"
OR DEAD.

MARY PETTIBONE POOLE

When people tell you how young you look, they are also telling you how old you are.

CARY GRANT

When did
your ears
become
hairier than
your head?

AT MIDDLE AGE
THE SOUL SHOULD
BE OPENING UP
LIKE A ROSE,
**NOT CLOSING
UP LIKE A
CABBAGE.**

JOHN ANDREW HOLMES

The secret to staying young is to live honestly, eat slowly and lie about your age.

Lucille Ball

Don't let ageing get you down. It's too hard to get back up.

John Wagner

OLD AGE AIN'T NO PLACE FOR SISSIES.

Bette Davis

WE DON'T GROW OLDER, WE GROW RIPER.

PABLO PICASSO

OLD AGE IS ALWAYS FIFTEEN YEARS OLDER THAN I AM.

BERNARD BARUCH

YOU'RE NOT REALLY OLD UNTIL YOU BECOME FOSSILIZED — SO JUST KEEP MOVING!

INSIDE EVERY
OLDER PERSON IS
A YOUNGER PERSON
WONDERING WHAT
THE HELL HAPPENED.

CORA HARVEY ARMSTRONG

The idea is to die young as late as possible.

Ashley Montagu

YOU KNOW
YOU'RE
GETTING OLD
WHEN FARTS
BECOME
INVOLUNTARY.

My idea of Hell is to
be young again.

MARGE PIERCY

Autumn is mellower, and what we lose in flowers, we more than gain in fruits.

Samuel Butler

I REFUSE TO ADMIT
I'M MORE THAN 52,
**EVEN IF THAT
DOES MAKE
MY SONS
ILLEGITIMATE.**

NANCY ASTOR

You're not old; you're "new and improved".

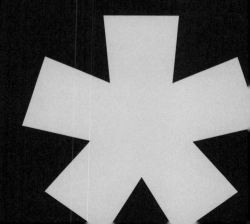

You're in pretty good shape for the shape you are in!

Dr Seuss

YOU DON'T GET OLDER, YOU GET BETTER.

Shirley Bassey

REMEMBER: OLD AGE IS JUST A NUMBER. SO WHAT IF IT'S QUITE A BIG NUMBER?

OLD PEOPLE
SHOULDN'T
EAT HEALTH
FOODS. THEY
NEED ALL THE
PRESERVATIVES
THEY CAN GET.

ROBERT ORBEN

PEOPLE WHO SAY YOU'RE JUST AS OLD AS YOU FEEL ARE ALL WRONG, FORTUNATELY.

RUSSELL BAKER

I WASTED TIME,
AND NOW DOTH
TIME WASTE ME.

WILLIAM SHAKESPEARE

The memory loss will save you a fortune in Christmas cards.

THE OLDER I GET, THE OLDER OLD IS.

TOM BAKER

Youth would be an ideal state
if it came a little later in life.

H. H. ASQUITH

At your age you need glasses – wine glasses, sherry glasses, gin glasses, whisky glasses...

YOU KNOW
YOU'RE GETTING
OLD WHEN "GETTING
SOME ACTION"
MOSTLY INVOLVES
**BUYING
LAXATIVES.**

As for me,
except for an
occasional
heart attack,
I feel as young
as I ever did.

Robert Benchley

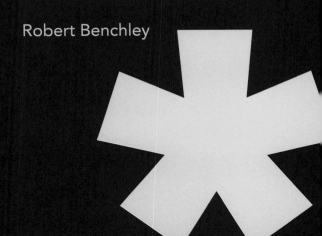

They tell you that you'll lose your mind when you grow older. What they don't tell you is that you won't miss it very much.

Malcolm Cowley

THE FEWER F*CKS YOU GIVE ABOUT GETTING OLDER, THE HAPPIER YOU'LL BE!

I'M TOO OLD FOR A PAPER ROUND, TOO YOUNG FOR SOCIAL SECURITY AND TOO TIRED FOR AN AFFAIR.

ERMA BOMBECK

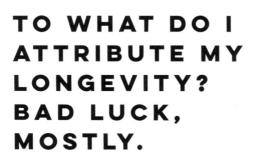

TO WHAT DO I
ATTRIBUTE MY
LONGEVITY?
BAD LUCK,
MOSTLY.

BILLY WILDER

THE OLDER YOU GET, THE MORE YOU ENJOY STAYING AT HOME AND DOING F*CK ALL.

I SAID TO MY HUSBAND, "MY BOOBS HAVE GONE, MY STOMACH'S GONE, SAY SOMETHING NICE ABOUT MY LEGS." HE SAID, "BLUE GOES WITH EVERYTHING."

JOAN RIVERS

These days it's more easy listening than *Easy Rider.*

I'M PLEASED
TO BE HERE.
LET'S FACE
IT, AT MY
AGE I'M VERY
PLEASED TO BE
ANYWHERE.

GEORGE BURNS

Live your life and
forget your age.

Life begins at 40 – but so do fallen arches, rheumatism, faulty eyesight, and the tendency to tell a story to the same person three or four times.

William Feather

I INTEND TO LIVE FOREVER.
SO FAR, SO GOOD.

STEVEN WRIGHT

It's never too late to get your sh*t together.

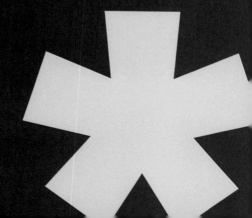

Like a lot of fellows around here, I have a furniture problem. My chest has fallen into my drawers.

Billy Casper

THE OLDER I GET, THE BETTER I USED TO BE.

Lee Trevino

I'M HAPPY TO REPORT THAT MY INNER CHILD IS STILL AGELESS.

JAMES BROUGHTON

YOU KNOW YOU'RE GETTING OLD WHEN THE LARGE PRINT SECTION OF THE LIBRARY SUDDENLY SEEMS VERY APPEALING.

I'M AT AN
AGE WHERE
MY BACK GOES
OUT MORE
THAN I DO.

PHYLLIS DILLER

A MAN LOSES HIS ILLUSIONS FIRST, HIS TEETH SECOND, AND HIS FOLLIES LAST.

HELEN ROWLAND

They say after the age of 20 you lose 70 million brain cells per year. You must have gone through two brains in your lifetime.

AS YOU GET OLDER, THE PICKINGS GET SLIMMER, BUT THE PEOPLE SURE DON'T.

CARRIE FISHER

You know you're getting
old when a four-letter word
for something pleasurable
two people can do in bed
together is R-E-A-D.

DENIS NORDEN

How do I confront ageing? With a wonder and a terror.

Keanu Reeves

YOUR BIRTHDAY
CAKES ARE
BECOMING A
**SERIOUS FIRE
HAZARD.**

I think people would live a bit longer if they didn't know how old they were.

Karl Pilkington

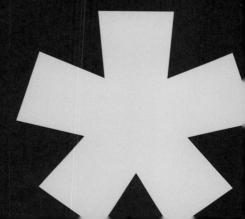

Years may wrinkle the skin, but to give up enthusiasm wrinkles the soul.

Samuel Ullman

WHAT'S
BETTER
THAN A
NIGHT OUT?

A CANCELLED
NIGHT OUT.

I DON'T FEEL 80. IN FACT, I DON'T FEEL ANYTHING UNTIL NOON, THEN IT'S TIME FOR MY NAP.

BOB HOPE

THE GREAT THING ABOUT GETTING OLDER IS THAT YOU DON'T LOSE ALL THE OTHER AGES YOU'VE BEEN.

MADELEINE L'ENGLE

AFTER A CERTAIN NUMBER OF YEARS OUR FACES BECOME OUR BIOGRAPHIES.

CYNTHIA OZICK

YOU KNOW YOU'RE OLD WHEN YOU'RE STILL WORKING OFF THE HANGOVER FROM A MONTH AGO.

I plan on growing old much later in life, or maybe not at all.

Patty Carey

WHEN YOU ARE
DISSATISFIED
AND WOULD
LIKE TO GO
BACK TO YOUR
YOUTH... THINK
OF ALGEBRA.

WILL ROGERS

Your childhood punishments become your goals as you get older: going to bed early, staying at home and not going to parties.

That's the privilege of old age: you don't have to remember.

Alan Arkin

THE EXCITEMENT
OF LEARNING
SEPARATES YOUTH
FROM OLD AGE.
**AS LONG AS
YOU'RE LEARNING,
YOU'RE NOT OLD.**

ROSALYN SUSSMAN YALOW

If you don't have wrinkles, you haven't laughed enough.

Phyllis Diller

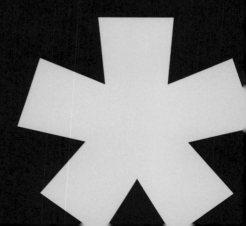

Young at heart...
slightly older in
other places.

FOR US
ELDERLY
PEOPLE, NOT
OWNING A
COMPUTER
IS LIKE NOT
HAVING A
HEADACHE.

Edward Enfield

I CAN STILL ENJOY SEX AT 74. I LIVE AT 75, SO IT'S NO DISTANCE.

BOB MONKHOUSE

MIRROR,
MIRROR ON
THE WALL.
I AM MY
PARENTS
AFTER ALL.

OLD AGE IS THE ONLY THING THAT LIVES UP TO ITS REPUTATION.

EMILY LEVINE

I LOVE GETTING OLDER.
THEN AGAIN, I NEVER
PUT MY GLASSES ON
BEFORE LOOKING IN
THE MIRROR.

CHERIE LUNGHI

The really frightening thing about middle age is the knowledge that you'll grow out of it.

Doris Day

YOU'RE STILL THE LIFE OF THE PARTY (EVEN IF YOU'RE THE FIRST TO LEAVE).

Old age is like learning a new profession. And not one of your own choosing.

JACQUES BARZUN

Ageing is an extraordinary process where you become the person you always should have been.

David Bowie

YOU KNOW
YOU'RE GETTING
OLD WHEN
YOU REALIZE
YOUR PARENTS
WERE RIGHT
ALL ALONG.

I'd be more inclined to grow up if I saw it worked out for everyone else.

Anonymous

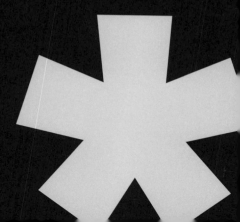

**To stop ageing –
keep on raging.**

Michael Forbes

WE ARE ONLY YOUNG ONCE. THAT IS ALL SOCIETY CAN STAND.

Bob Bowen

WITH OLD AGE COMES NEW SKILLS... SOON YOU WILL BE ABLE TO COUGH, LAUGH AND PEE ALL AT THE SAME TIME!

I HAVE REACHED
AN AGE WHERE
IF SOMEONE
TELLS ME TO
WEAR SOCKS,
I DON'T HAVE TO.

ALBERT EINSTEIN

AGE IS A NECESSARY BUT INSUFFICIENT REQUIREMENT FOR GROWING UP.

HENRY CLOUD

AS YOU GET OLDER,
IT'S IMPORTANT TO
STAY FLEXIBLE...
ABOUT YOUR AGE.

Young people don't know what age is, and old people forget what youth was.

Irish proverb

I KNOW I CAN'T CHEAT DEATH, BUT I CAN CHEAT OLD AGE.

DARWIN DEASON

There are some people who imagine that older adults don't know how to use the internet. My immediate reaction is, "I've got news for you: we invented it."

VINT CERF

A little age adds a lot of flavour.

YOU CAN
ALWAYS
BE TRUSTED
WITH SECRETS
**BECAUSE
YOU NEVER
REMEMBER
THEM.**

There is only one cure for grey. It was invented by a Frenchman. It is called the guillotine.

P. G. Wodehouse

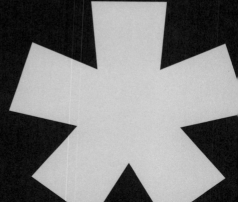

You're not getting old; you're just getting started.

OLD AGE IS LIKE EVERYTHING ELSE. TO MAKE A SUCCESS OF IT, YOU'VE GOT TO START YOUNG.

Anonymous

THE TROUBLE WITH RETIREMENT IS THAT YOU NEVER GET A DAY OFF.

ABE LEMONS

WHEN I WAS A BOY, THE DEAD SEA WAS ONLY SICK.

GEORGE BURNS

I CONSIDERED
WORKING OUT
BUT THEN I
REALIZED
THIS NAP
WASN'T GOING
TO TAKE ITSELF.

RETIRED IS BEING TIRED TWICE... FIRST TIRED OF WORKING, THEN TIRED OF NOT.

RICHARD ARMOUR

I have now gotten to the age when I must prove that I'm just as good as I never was.

Rex Harrison

DO NOT WORRY ABOUT AVOIDING TEMPTATION. AS YOU GROW OLDER IT WILL AVOID YOU.

JOEY ADAMS

Time is a dressmaker
specializing in alterations.

FAITH BALDWIN

Professionally, I have no age.

Kathleen Turner

IN YOUTH
WE RUN INTO
DIFFICULTIES.
**IN OLD AGE
DIFFICULTIES
RUN INTO US.**

JOSH BILLINGS

How old would you be if you didn't know how old you were?

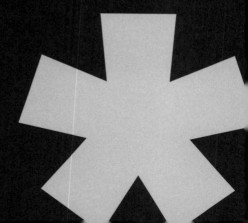

It takes a
long time to
grow young.

AS I GET
OLDER, I
CAN SENSE
PEOPLE
DRESSING
ME WITH
THEIR EYES.

Anonymous

WINE AND FRIENDS IMPROVE WITH AGE.

THE OLDER ONE GROWS, THE MORE ONE LIKES INDECENCY.

VIRGINIA WOOLF

THE FIRST SIGN OF MATURITY IS THE DISCOVERY THAT THE VOLUME KNOB ALSO TURNS TO THE LEFT.

JERRY M. WRIGHT

MY GRANDMOTHER
IS OVER 80 AND STILL
DOESN'T NEED GLASSES.
DRINKS RIGHT OUT
OF THE BOTTLE.

HENNY YOUNGMAN

You were born
to be wild...
but only
till 9 p.m.

THERE'S NOTHING WRONG WITH YOU THAT REINCARNATION WON'T CURE.

JACK E. LEONARD

I was getting dressed
and a peeping Tom looked
in the window, took a look
and pulled down the shade.

JOAN RIVERS

You know
you're getting
older when
you stop
treating the
speed limit
as a target.

I STILL THINK OF MYSELF AS I WAS 25 YEARS AGO. **THEN I LOOK IN THE MIRROR AND SEE AN OLD BASTARD AND I REALIZE IT'S ME.**

DAVE ALLEN

Life really does begin at 40. Up until then you are just doing research.

Carl Jung

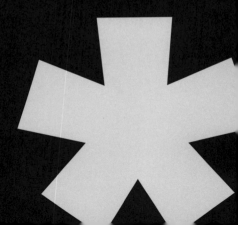

At your age people expect you to be calm, sophisticated and sober. Disappoint them.

YOU KNOW
YOU'RE
GETTING
OLDER
IF YOU
HAVE MORE
FINGERS
THAN REAL
TEETH.

Rodney Dangerfield

OLD AGE COMES ON SUDDENLY, AND NOT GRADUALLY AS IS THOUGHT.

EMILY DICKINSON

**F*CK
YOU'RE
OLD!**